JAKE AND JEN
in the Night of the Ninja

Written by Chris Bradford

Illustrated by Korky Paul

Collins

"Did you hear that strange sound?" asked Jake Jones, chief protector of the Emperor of Japan.

Jen peered into the castle courtyard. "It's just your imagination."

Jake pulled out his bokken. "I swore I heard something unusual. What if it's a ninja?"

"Our instructions are to keep the treasure safe for the Emperor," replied Jen. "We must obey."

Jen edged round the courtyard, while Jake trudged in the other direction. They met under a large cherry blossom tree.

"Did you spot anyone?" asked Jen.

Jake shook his head. "The Emperor's precious hoard is still safe."

Then they both heard a rattling sound.

Jake gnawed on his fingernails. "What's that? A ninja?"

Jen's expression turned suspicious. "Sounds more like an insect ..."

Jake spotted a strange shadow in the tree.
"There! I caught sight of the ninja!"

But when Jen peered up, there was nothing to see.

Jake's knees knocked together. "I'm scared!"

"Calm down," sneered Jen. "You need to be brave."

"But ninjas are known to be dangerous," said Jake. "They can climb up sheer walls. They can change shape into ferocious animals. They can soar like bats. They can disappear like phantoms. They can even stop your pulse with one touch!"

Jen laughed. "Those are just myths."

Then two grey eyes stared straight at her and Jen stopped laughing. "Ninja!" she squealed.

Jake lunged at the ninja.

The ninja dodged aside and leapt over them as if weightless. He knocked Jake on the head.

Jake fell to his knees. He clutched his sore skull.

"I think I have concussion!"

Jen tore after the ninja who was on a mission to snatch the treasure.

Inside the castle the ninja suddenly changed course.
Jen careered round the corner after the ninja.

"Ow! Ow! Ow!" she cried, shifting her weight from one foot to the other.

The floorboards were covered in vicious spikes which pricked her sandals.

As she edged around the trap, Jen lost the ninja.
Jake crawled in on his knees. "The Emperor is
in danger!"

Knowing the ninja was about to lunge, they both plunged through the paper wall.

They caught the ninja. But the ninja gnashed its teeth and swiped at Jen.

"HEY!" yelled Jen, enraged, as the naughty ninja escaped.

Then the lights came on!

"What is our daughter doing there?" cried Bella's parents.

Jake and Jen's baby cousin sat on the edge of the sideboard. She had a handful of sweets and was eating them with great pleasure.

Straight-faced, Jake and Jen pointed in the direction of their older brother.

"Shane!" roared their mother. "Your instructions were to babysit your cousin, not play video games on the television!"

Shane surveyed the mess in the lounge. He was given the chore of tidying up for not obeying his mother.

"Bella sure made a good ninja," laughed Jake as he changed out of his cardboard armour.

Jen peered up at the dark smudge hiding on the bookshelf and sucked her sore thumb. "Yes, but there's an even more dangerous ninja here — our cat!"

Ninja

skill: ninjutsu

main role: spy

Emperor's protector

skill: military training

main role: keeping
the Emperor safe

Spot the ninjas

How many ninjas can you spot?

27

Ninja star

How to fold a paper ninja star.

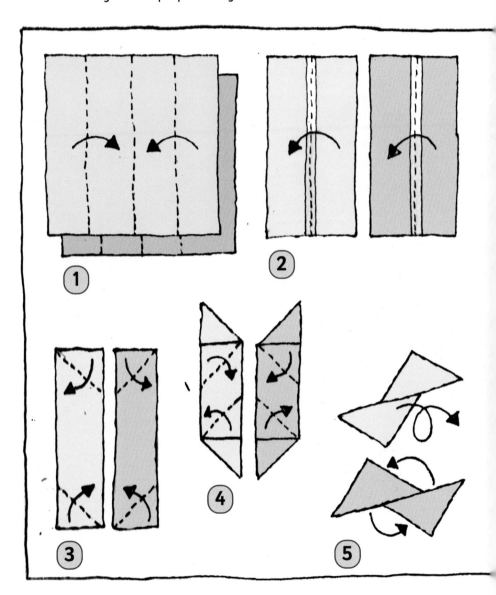

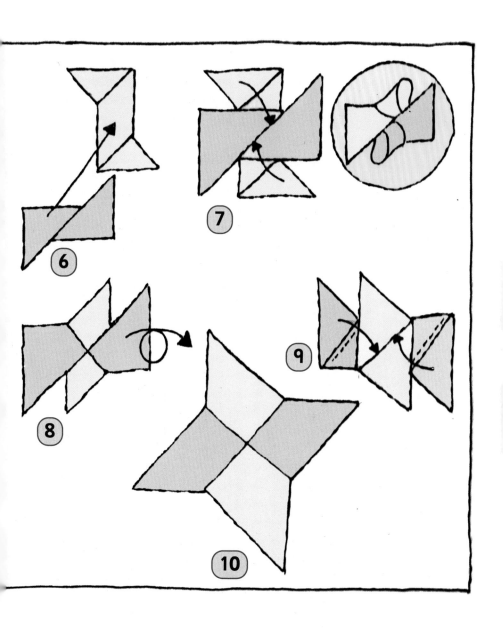

6

7

8

9

10

Ninja mission

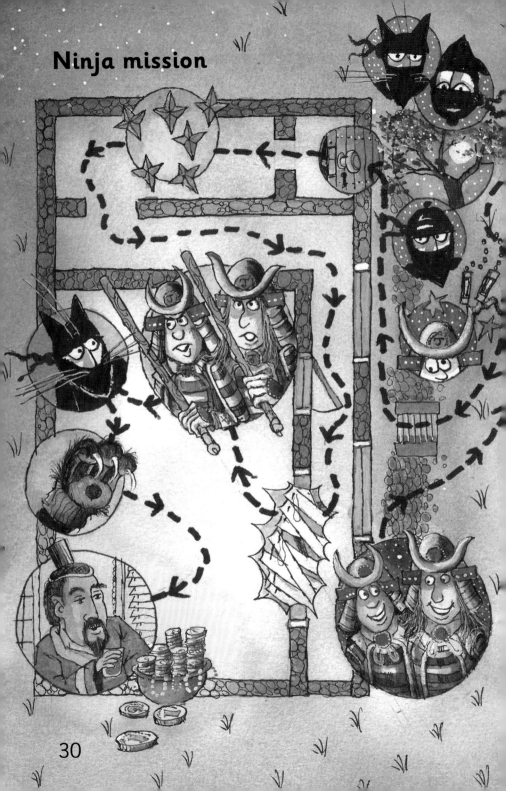

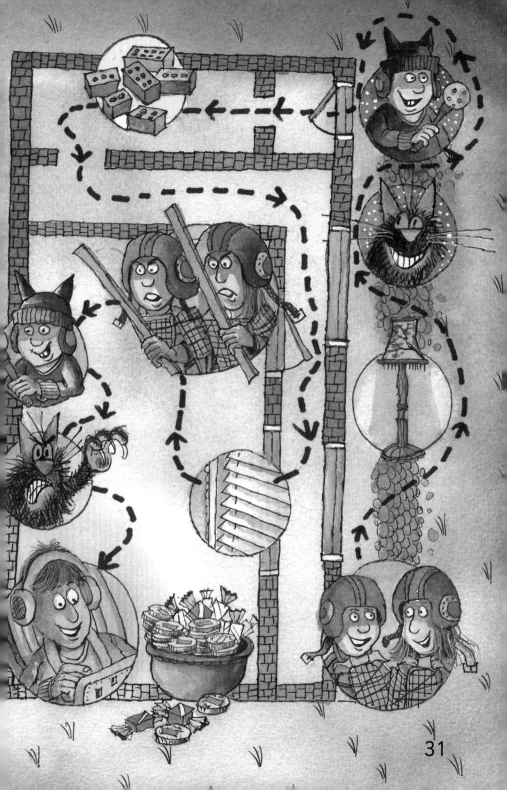

 Review: After reading

Use your assessment from hearing the children read to choose any GPCs, words or tricky words that need additional practice.

Read 1: Decoding
- Turn to pages 10 and 11. Ask the children to find as many different spellings of the /ai/ sound as possible. (**grey, straight, weightless**) Repeat for /or/ on pages 20 and 21. (**daughter, sideboard, roared, your**)
- Challenge the children to take turns to read a paragraph fluently. Say: Try to blend any unfamiliar words in your head before reading them aloud.

Read 2: Prosody
- Turn to pages 8 and 9. Ask the children to work in pairs and take turns to read Jen and Jake's spoken words as if for a radio play.
- For page 8, say: Think about how Jen's voice might sound. Can you speak in a sneering voice?
- For page 9, say: Do you think Jake is really scared, or is he enjoying the thrill and trying to scare Jen? Which words might he emphasise? (e.g. *the scariest words:* **dangerous, sheer, ferocious, soar, phantoms, stop, one touch**)

Read 3: Comprehension
- Encourage the children to compare this story with any other "Jake and Jen" stories they have read, or stories about ninjas they are familiar with.
- Point to the last sentence on page 2: **It's just your imagination.** Ask: How far is this true for everything that happens to Jake and Jen? What are the clues?
- Point to these words on pages 4 and 5, and ask the children what they mean in the context of the story:
  edged (e.g. *moved gradually*)
  spot (e.g. *catch sight of, see*)
  hoard (e.g. *guarded collection of something valuable*)
- Turn to pages 30 and 31. Working in two groups, ask one group to retell the story, while the other explains what is really happening at each stage. Prompt the second group by asking:
  o Who are the **ninjas**, really? (*Bella and the cat*); Who is the Emperor? (*Shane*)
  o What is the **cherry blossom tree**? (*a lamp*); What are the **vicious spikes**? (plastic *bricks*)
- Bonus content: Turn to pages 26 and 27 and invite the children to talk about what they can see in the picture before counting the ninjas (there are 30).